TABLE OF CONTENTS

Novel-Ties® are printed on recycled paper.

For the Teacher

This reproducible study guide consists of lessons to use in conjunction with the book *Sadako and the Thousand Paper Cranes*. Written in chapter-by-chapter format, the guide contains a synopsis, pre-reading activities, vocabulary and comprehension exercises, as well as extension activities to be used as follow-up to the book.

In a homogeneous classroom, whole class instruction with one title is appropriate. In a heterogeneous classroom, reading groups should be formed: each group works on a different novel on its reading level. Depending upon the length of time devoted to reading in the classroom, each novel, with its guide and accompanying lessons, may be completed in three to six weeks.

Begin using NOVEL-TIES for guided reading by distributing the novel and a folder to each child. Distribute duplicated pages of the study guide for students to place in their folders. After examining the cover and glancing through the book, students can participate in several pre-reading activities. Vocabulary questions should be considered prior to reading a chapter or group of chapters; all other work should be done after the chapter has been read. Comprehension questions can be answered orally or in writing. The classroom teacher should determine the amount of work to be assigned, always keeping in mind that readers must be nurtured and that the ultimate goal is encouraging students' love of reading.

The benefits of using NOVEL-TIES are numerous. Students read good literature in the original, rather than in abridged or edited form. The good reading habits will be transferred to the books students read independently. Passive readers become active, avid readers.

POST-READING ACTIVITIES AND QUESTIONS

1. Reread the Prologue to the novel and explain why you think the author wrote this book. Although the book was first published in 1977, do you think the issues it raises are important today?

2. Imagine that you are one of Sadako's classmates. Design a memorial for her. Create a short poem or find one that has already been written that could accompany this memorial.

3. There is a great deal of debate today on the value of nuclear weapons and the concept of a "nuclear freeze." Debate these issues with your classmates. Did this book influence your opinions on these subjects?

4. What do you think the author is really trying to say about human courage and humanity's power to destroy itself?

5. The Japanese have a unique way of looking at life. They derive great joy from finding beauty in small, simple things. Scan the book and find at least three such things that were beautiful to the Sasaki family.

6. The food eaten by the Sasaki family is different from Western food. Make a wall chart showing the contrast between a typical Japanese meal and a Western meal. Make the chart artistic and interesting by using drawings or photographic illustrations as well as captions.

7. Do some research to learn about the religions of Japan. Describe Buddhism and Shintoism and tell how they differ from major Western religions.

8. **Art Connection:** In Chapter Seven there is an illustration of a kokeshi doll. Take a bar of soap or a piece of balsa wood and carve a small kokeshi doll. You could use bright red, yellow, or blue paint for the base and black for the hair.

9. Did you like the ending of this story? Would the story have been better or worse if the author changed the true story and had Sadako live at the end?

10. Even though Sadako never finished making one thousand cranes and she died at the end of the story, do you feel that this is a depressing or an uplifting story?

HAIKU

Haiku is a form of poetry that has been practiced in Japan since the 1400s. Each poem contains approximately seventeen syllables and is written in three lines. There are usually five syllables in the first line, seven syllables in the second line, and five syllables in the third line. The lines do not rhyme and the subject is usually found in nature. Japanese writers of haiku believe that the smallest thing in nature can become precious if one takes the time to look at it carefully. Each poem presents one idea in one simple observation.

Look carefully at the example of a haiku at the end of Chapter Five in *Sadako and the Thousand Paper Cranes*. Although it does not exactly fit the 5-7-5 syllable pattern, it does meet the other qualifications.

- What is being described? _____

- What thought is expressed? _____

_____

- What mood does it create? _____

_____

Issa was an eighteenth-century Japanese poet renowned for his haiku. Here are some examples of his poems translated into English. He is said to have written the first one when he was only nine years old.

Please come
Motherless sparrows
And play with me.

The spider's children
Scatter in all directions
To make their own way.

A single nest
Beneath an old pine tree
Makes a summer house.

With these examples as a guide, write your own haiku. Use observations of the world or your own experience. These poems could be illustrated with simple line drawings or watercolor paintings.

HOW TO MAKE AN ORIGAMI PAPER CRANE

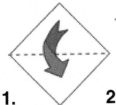

1.

Start with a standard 8-1/2 x 11 inch sheet of paper and then cut it into a square. Fold the square in half diagonally.

2.

Fold in half from right to left diagonally again.

3.

Spread the pocket out from the inside and fold to make a small square.

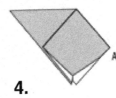

4.

Your paper should look like this. Now turn it over to start step 5.

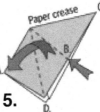

5.

Fold Point B onto Point A, while at the same time folding the paper crease inward so that Point C is touching Point D.

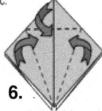

6.

Here's the tricky part. Fold left and right corners toward the center line along the diagonal dotted line and then fold the top corner along the dotted line.

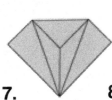

7.

Note: The folds from step 6 are only to create a crease.

Your Paper should look like this.

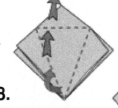

8.

Now open the pocket by pulling the bottom corner up and fold inward along the crease. Some creases will become inverted.

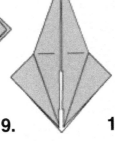

9.

The figure should look like this. Be careful to score the edges and corners cleanly. Turn over and repeat Steps 6-8.

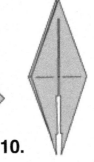

10.

Fold in the lower flaps made in Step 9. Now you're half way done and have the base.

11.

Making sure you have the right side up, fold side corners in toward the middle along the dotted lines.

12.

The figure should look like this. Turn over.

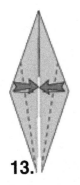

13.

Do the same as Step 11.

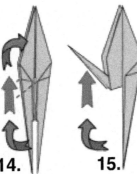

14.

Reverse fold at dotted lines to form the head.

15.

Slightly open the side and bring the head part up like this.

16.

Bring up at this point and press down. Do the same to form the tail on the other side.

17.

Reverse fold at dotted lines to form the beak. You can select the length of the beak.

18.

Bend the wings down and out into the proper position. You can bow in from the bottom.

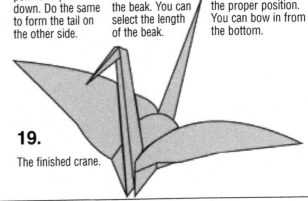

19.

The finished crane.

SUGGESTIONS FOR FURTHER READING

    Bang, Molly. *The Paper Crane*. Greenwillow.

*   Bauer, Marion D. *On My Honor*. HMH Books.

*   Buck, Pearl S. *The Big Wave*. HarperCollins.

    Choi, Yanasook. *The Name Jar*. Dragonfly.

*   Fox, Paula. *One-Eyed Cat*. Dell.

    Friedman, Ina R. *How My Parents Learned to Eat*. HMH Books.

    Harbin, Robert. *Origami: The Art of Paperfolding*. Perennial.

*   Huynh, Quang Nhuong. *The Land I Lost*. Harper.

    Issa, Kobayashi. *Issa: Cup-of-Tea Poems*. Asian Humanities Press.

    Lachenmeyer, Nathaniel. *The Origami Master*. Albert Whitman.

*   Naidoo, Beverly. *Journey to Jo'burg*. HarperCollins.

*   Paterson, Katherine. *Bridge to Terabithia*. HarperCollins.

    _____. *The Master Puppeteer*. HarperCollins.

    _____. *Of Nightingales that Weep*. HarperCollins.

*   _____. *Park's Quest*. Puffin.

    _____. *The Sign of the Chrysanthemum*. HarperCollins.

    Say, Allen. *Tree of Cranes*. HMH Books.

*   Smith, Doris. *A Taste of Blackberries*. HarperCollins.

    Stein, Conrad R. *Hiroshima, World at War*. Childrens Press.

    Sumiko, Yagawa. *The Crane Wife*. HMH Books.

    Takayuki, Ishii. *One Thousand Paper Cranes*. Laurel Leaf.

Some Other Books by Eleanor Coerr

* *The Big Balloon Race*. HarperCollins.

* *Chang's Paper Pony*. HarperCollins.

* *The Josefina Story Quilt*. HarperCollins.

Lady With a Torch. HarperCollins.

Mieko and the Fifth Treasure. Putnam.

*   NOVEL-TIES Study Guides are available for these titles.

ANSWER KEY

Vocabulary I: 1. fidgeted – moved around restlessly 2. ancestors – people in your family who lived before you were born 3. leukemia – disease of the blood in which there are too many white blood corpuscles 4. shrines –places sacred to the memory of someone who died 5. throngs – crowds gathered together

Vocabulary II: 1. b   2. g   3. c   4. e   5. d   6. a   7. f   8. h;   1. qualify   2. wistful   3. parasol   4. stern   5. origami   6. omen   7. flustered   8. tatami

Prologue, Chapters 1 - 3

Questions: 1. Sadako was twelve years old when she died. 2. The United States of America dropped the atomic bomb in an attempt to end World War II by forcing the Japanese to surrender. 3. The atom bomb disease was leukemia. It was feared nine years after the bomb was dropped because radiation that entered the body might not manifest itself until years later. 4. Sadako's mother became angry when her daughter referred to the August 6th celebration as a carnival because that was the day on which the atom bomb was dropped on Hiroshima. It was primarily a memorial day. 5. Breakfast consisted of rice, soup, and pickled radishes. Answers to the second part of the question will vary. 6. The family prayed for the well-being of their dead relatives in their afterlife. 7. Sadako was very energetic and always in a hurry. She was a good runner, an obedient girl, a good sister, and friend. She practiced hard to get what she wanted and did not complain when things did not go her way. She was an optimistic person. 8. Sadako and Chizuko were best friends, but they did not agree on everything. 9. At the Peace Park on August 6th, there were speeches by Buddhist priests and the mayor. Doves, the traditional symbols of peace, were released above the Atomic Dome. People walked through the memorial buildings to view photographs of Hiroshima after the atom bomb. On a lighter note, there were games and races for the children and specialty foods were sold. In the evening, paper lanterns commemorating the dead were floated on the Ohta River. 10. Masahiro timed Sadako with their father's big watch and the whole family came to watch Sadako run and cheer her on. 11. Sadako first began to feel ill on the day of the big race. It was after the race was won that she felt strange and dizzy for the first time.

Chapters 4 - 9 and Epilogue

Questions: 1. Sadako was taken to the hospital because she collapsed at the race. She was frightened of the hospital because she knew that many patients were victims of the atom bomb disease. Answers to the last part of the question will vary. 2. Chizuko showed Sadako how to make origami paper cranes to make her believe that she would get well again. Sadako felt safe with the little golden crane by her side. 3. Sadako spent much of her time folding paper cranes in order to keep up her courage. She also did her homework and wrote letters. 4. Paper folding kept Sadako busy and gave her hope. It also gave her parents a sense of purpose. 5. Sadako felt she needed to cheer up Kenji because he had no family to comfort and visit him. 6. Mrs. Sasaki was not able to do much to help her daughter. The present of food was more of a symbolic gesture than a real gift. She brought chicken and rice, pickled plums, and bean cakes. Sadako was too sick to eat the food. 7. Sadako rallied enough to make a visit home. 0 Bon, the most important holiday in Japan, is a celebration for spirits of the dead who return to visit those who loved them on earth. 8. Sadako felt weak and sick after a day of visitors not home. She longed for the quiet and care she received at the hospital. 9. The description of Sadako's death at the end of the book showed her slipping peacefully into death. 10. A collection of Sadako's letters was published and there is a statue at the Peace Park to commemorate Sadako Sosudis life.